EFFECT SIZE MATTERS

How Reporting and Interpreting Effect Sizes
Can Improve your Publication Prospects and
Make the World a Better Place!

Mad Methods .co

PAUL D. ELLIS

Effect Size Matters:
How Reporting and Interpreting Effect Sizes Can Improve your
Publication Prospects and Make the World a Better Place!

ISBN: 978-1-927230-56-5

Published by MadMethods, an imprint of KingsPress.org,
PO Box 66145, Beach Haven, Auckland 0749, New Zealand.

To get this title in other formats and to find other titles in the
MadMethods series, visit www.MadMethods.co

Version: 1.2 (September 2020)

Dedication: For my students.

What readers are saying about
The Essential Guide to Effect Sizes

I actually emailed friends to tell them I was excited that this book was on my summer reading list. I'm enjoying it very much!

— Amazon Reviewer

Excellent book that clearly explains the concepts behind statistical mechanics. Easy to read.

— John Frias Morales

Given the increasing recognition of the limitations of standard null-hypothesis significance tests, I find all the topics covered in the book important as they indicate ways how we can substantially improve the interpretation of our empirical research results. I would recommend this book to scholars, doctoral students, and practitioners interested in the advanced interpretation of empirical research findings.

— Andreas Schwab

I was impressed by the clarity (and very amusing examples) in this text.

— Amazon Reviewer

Outstanding and easy to understand reference. Inordinately helpful.

— William Jacobson

I've recommended this book to other grad students in my classes. It's a short read with a ton of good stuff in it. It doesn't try to teach you everything about statistics, but it does a good job of teaching you how to think responsibly with statistics.

An easy read on a complex topic. Great resource!

"Statistical significance is the least interesting thing about the results. You should describe the results in terms of measures of magnitude—not just, does a treatment affect people, but how much does it affect them."

— Gene Glass, quoted in Hunt (1997: 29–30)

Contents

Why do I
need this book?

Science, in essence, comprises two activities: (1) discovering new stuff and (2) whacking it with a hammer to see what happens. This book is for the hammer-whackers. It's for those of us trying to figure out why things work the way they do.

If your job is to learn how some *thing* affects some other *thing,* this book is for you. Specifically, it's for those who want to know the effect of X on Y, regardless of whether we are talking about:

- the effect of a treatment on some outcome
- the effect of a strategy on performance
- the effect of a crisis on decision-making
- the effect of an intervention on addiction
- the effect of advertising on behavior
- the effect of a drug on mental health
- the effect of an innovation on standards of living
- the effect of a vaccine on the spread of a disease

Perhaps you are not used to thinking of yourself as a researcher of effects (or a hammer-whacker). I certainly didn't. Like most researchers I began my career with a tool box full of techniques for crunching data and testing hypotheses. I lived and died on the results of statistical tests. Those tools are useful, but they are just tools. They are not the main thing.

So, what is the main thing?

Whether you test hypotheses or not, whether you crunch data or don't, the main thing is to move towards a better understanding of real world effects.

An effect may be the result of a researcher's intervention or an act of nature. It could be the outcome of a plan, a process, or a collision with an iceberg. An effect may be desirable or undesirable, anticipated or surprising. It may be a one-off occurrence or it may happen every day of the week and twice on Sundays.

Effects are the stuff of life and stuff happens.

What do researchers do? We study effects. Your specific field of interest may be medicine, education, economics, communications, geography, political science, psychology, sociology, social work, management, marketing, linguistics, epidemiology, international relations, industrial relations, development studies, environmental studies, information science, or zymurgy, but you are in the business of estimating effect sizes.

Researchers estimate effect sizes in order to interpret their meaning and make sense of the world we live in.

In this book, you will learn these two essential skills—how to estimate and interpret effect sizes. In Part A, we will look at different ways to estimate the size of an effect; in Part B, we will look at different ways to interpret and draw conclusions from our estimates.

Five reasons to read this book

There are at least five reasons why researchers ought to be interested in effect sizes:

1. Effect sizes, not p-values, are the primary output of your study. Your estimate of the effect size constitutes your study's evidence. Since you spent months or years looking for it, it would be sense-less not to report it. A study that doesn't report effect sizes is as convincing as a prosecution case with no witnesses. The prosecutor may tell a good story, but without evidence he's just wasting time. This point bears repeating: your estimate of the effect size is your evidence. Without it, your research is incomplete.

2. The estimation of effect sizes is essential to the interpretation of a study's results. Practical take-aways based on p values tend to be vague and speculative. In contrast, reporting the effect size facilitates the explicit interpretation of the sub-stantive or practical significance of a result.

11

3. Reporting effect sizes prevents you re-inventing the wheel. By comparing effect size estimates obtained in different settings, researchers can better identify prospective lines of enquiry while avoiding investigative dead ends.

4. Reporting and interpreting effect sizes improves your publication prospects. Journal editors are increasingly insisting on the reporting of effect sizes in their guidelines for prospective authors. These calls are being made in every discipline, from education to rehabilitation, and from psychology to business studies. We would be wise to anticipate a future where studies that don't report effect sizes are routinely given desk rejects. Researchers who learn how to report and interpret effect sizes will benefit from these changing publication policies.

5. In many disciplines there is an ongoing push towards relevance and engagement with stakeholders beyond the research community. If our research is to make sense to practitioners and non-specialists, we need to abandon the time-worn habit of drawing large conclusions from small p values and engage directly with the evidence itself. We need to shift our focus from "did this test achieve statistical significance?" to "how big is the effect and what does it mean?" Research that makes sense will benefit society far more than

research no one reads or understands. The highly-cited researcher of tomorrow will be the one who seizes these emerging opportunities to explore new avenues of significance and meaning.

This book is not a text book. It's more of a rough and ready guide to a set of skills every researcher needs. It shouldn't take more than an hour or two to familiarize yourself with the concepts in this book.

Considering the potential returns on your investment, it will be a couple of hours well-spent.

Who wrote this book?

I'm a methods guy, but I never meant to be. As an undergrad, I found research methods and stats courses frighteningly difficult. I would get hung up on assumptions that seemed to make no sense, and I refused to be impressed by jargon.

Years later, through no fault of my own, I became a methods teacher. For 15 years I taught Research Methods to graduate student, and I enjoyed the challenge of being pushed by bright Ph.D. candidates.

At some point during this period I stumbled across effect sizes, and it was like my world turned upside-down. Or right-side up. I began to see that much of what I had been taught, and was now teaching, was incidental to the larger purposes of research. I had been taught to measure constructs and assess the veracity of hypotheses using tests of statistical significance, but I had never been taught how to estimate and interpret effect sizes.

Learning about effect sizes was the single best thing that ever happened to me as a researcher. Imagine a gold digger used to finding flakes and grains unearthing the 140 pound Welcome Stranger nugget. The fine flakes of what I had learned were still valuable; they just weren't as valuable as what I had now.

It was around about this time that I started getting recognition for my research—prizes, citations, even a medal. At one point I was rated the most prolific scholar in my field in the Asia-Pacific region. By all appearances, I was a successful scholar. But deep down, I was frustrated that I hadn't learned about effect sizes sooner.

How had I missed this?!

They say you don't learn anything until you teach it to others, so I began to pass on what I was learning about effect sizes. I began to teach meta-analysis and the analysis of statistical power in seminars. I developed the habit of reporting and interpreting effect sizes in my research papers. Serving on the editorial boards of several top tier journals, I began asking authors the same sorts of questions I was asking myself.

And then I wrote a book.

I wrote *The Essential Guide to Effect Sizes: Statistical Power, Meta-Analysis, and the Interpretation of Research Results* because I was frustrated with dense texts that struck me as unnecessarily complex and dense. It seemed that many of these books were written to impress rather than instruct. I saw an opportunity to write a jargon-free primer that covered all three legs of the effect size stool: meta-analysis, the analysis of statistical power, and the interpretation of effect sizes.

I sent *The Essential Guide* off to Cambridge University Press, and they published it.

Then... crickets.

I would like to say that the publication of my book revolutionized the world of research, but it didn't. Sales started out slow and only began to take off after a few years.

What was immediately successful, however, was a little website I put up to plug the book. Within a short time, the website received more than a million hits with traffic growing every month. The website is called www.effectsizefaq.com and it has some useful resources for researchers.

My textbook has everything you need to come to grips with effect sizes, but for some readers it may be too big a step into a strange new world. By gauging site visits, I have learned that most researchers are simply looking for answers to three questions:

(1) What is an effect size?
(2) How do I calculate the statistical power of my study?
(3) How do I draw definitive conclusions from inconclusive studies?

The book you are reading answers the first question. Two other books in the MadMethods series, *Statistical Power Trip* and *Meta-Analysis Made Easy*, answer the second and third questions respectively. (Value tip: You get three-books-in-one for a low price in the omnibus version.)

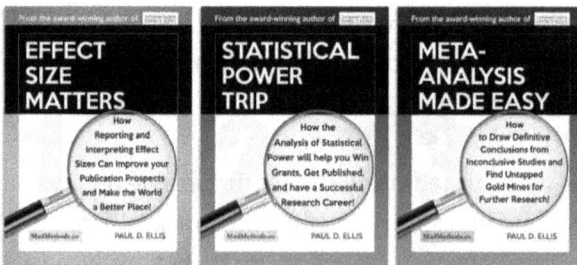

Why did I write these little books when I have already written a perfectly good text? Because students are poor and researchers are busy. You probably don't have six months to come to grips with these new subjects. You just want the short version.

Perhaps you have a deadline approaching or a reviewer breathing down your neck. Your attitude is, "I don't have time to read a dense text. I just wish someone could show me how to report and interpret effect sizes and quickly!"

Your wish is granted.

Paul D. Ellis

What is an effect size?

Let's begin with two definitions:

- An **effect** is the result of something. It is an outcome, a result, a reaction, a change in Y brought about by a change in X.

- An **effect size** refers to the magnitude of the outcome as it occurs, or would be found, in nature or in a population. Although effects can be observed in the artificial setting of a laboratory or a sample, effect sizes exist in the real world.

Table 1 contains a brief list of famous effects and the scientists who studied them.

Effect sizes are ubiquitous. You can find them in newspapers, college brochures, shop windows, Facebook ads, product packaging, church newsletters, blogs, tweets, TV commercials—just about anywhere.

Here are some everyday examples of effect size:

- lose 20 pounds in four weeks on the South Beach diet
- learn how to speak Swahili in six months
- make $2,300 a day working from home
- improve test performance through meditation

- fast-track your career with an MBA
- list your property with us and sell your home within a week
- read this book and improve your publication prospects

Table 1: Classic effects in science

How does this *X*...	...affect this *Y*?	Who?
gravity	celestial mechanics (and apples)	Isaac Newton (1680s)
cowpox vaccinations	smallpox immunity	Edward Jenner (1790s)
contaminated water	cholera outbreaks	John Snow (1850s)
alternating current	long distance transmission	Nikola Tesla (1880s)
semi-dwarf wheat	crop yields	Norman Borlaug (1950s)
aspirin	clotting diseases	Harvey Weiss (1960s)
bacteria	stomach ulcers	Barry Marshall (1980s)
legalized abortion	crime rates	Steven Levitt (1990s)
governance	economic development	Jeffrey Sachs (2000s)

All of these claims promise some sort of effect (a fast-tracked career, a sold home). Some even dare to promise effects of measurable size ("make $2,300 a day," "lose 20 pounds in four weeks"). No understanding of statistical significance is necessary to gauge the merits of these claims. Each is described in plain English using metrics that can be understood by just about anyone.

Every day we make decisions based on the analysis of effect sizes. We start diets because we believe they will help us to lose weight. We spend huge sums of money on education because we hope to earn higher incomes later. We buy books on effect sizes because we expect they will help us become better researchers.

The interpretation of effect sizes is how we make sense of the world.

We will return to the issue of interpretation in Part B. But first, we need to learn how to measure or estimate effect sizes.

How to estimate an effect size

Effects exist in the real world — in populations rather than laboratories. The best way to measure an effect is to conduct a census of an entire population. But as this is often not practicable, researchers typically estimate effects by observing representative samples. Thus we can distinguish effect sizes from our sample-based estimates of those effect sizes:

- effect sizes are real, extant, *out there*
- sample-based estimates of effect sizes are shadows or approximations of the real thing

Recall the Hindu tale of the blind men and the elephant (see Figure 1). None of the men had encountered an elephant before and groping about in their blindness each drew different conclusions.

The man touching the elephant's leg concluded, "An elephant is like a tree." "No," said the man touching the ear. "An elephant is like a fan." "You're both wrong," said the man holding the trunk. "An elephant is like a snake."[1]

---

[1] John Godfrey Saxe (1872), "The blind men and the elephant."

Figure 1: The blind men and the elephant

The elephant represents the effect size. It is what it is. The blind men represent researchers groping about with their sample-based studies. Each sample provides a snapshot of the elephant but doesn't necessarily give an accurate picture of the elephant as a whole. It is only when we put all the sample-based evidence together that the elephant begins to appear.

Since researchers with limited resources are like blind men, it is unwise to look at the results of a single study and conclude, "The effect size is exactly like this" or "The effect size is exactly this big." A safer conclusion would be as follows:

> Based on my results, I estimate the effect size is equivalent to $d = 0.45$. After reviewing estimates obtained from other studies in this area, I tentatively conclude that the effect size is likely to be within the 0.42–0.58 range.

This is a far more precise and reasonable conclusion than saying:

> I found a statistically significant result so there must be some effect. Since five out of eight previous studies found the same thing, I conclude that there is some positive relationship of unknown size. Those other three studies, which returned nonsignificant results, must've been done by sloppy researchers.

An illustration may help. About twenty years ago I did a study examining the effect of a market orientation on business performance. This is a very important effect because if being customer-oriented doesn't boost performance, what's the point of going to business school?

Happily, I found that a market orientation *does* have a positive effect on business performance. (Good news, B-Schools!) The more customer- and competitor-oriented you are, the better you will perform. But how big is this effect? Based on the results of my solitary study, I estimated the effect size to be equivalent to a correlation of $r = 0.25$ (Ellis 2007).

But here's the problem. My result was based on just one sample. There must be a million companies in the world and I only studied a few hundred of them. I was in danger of being the blind man who mistook elephants for trees.

To draw a more definitive conclusion, I needed to compare my study-specific estimate with estimates obtained in other studies. I did this by pooling published and unpublished effect sizes reported by others.

Altogether, I was able to identify 58 relevant studies with a combined sample size of 14,586 firms from 28 countries. When you think how many firms there in the world, this is still a drop in the bucket, but with this massive sample I was a lot closer to seeing the elephant.

From this combined set of studies I calculated a mean effect size of $\bar{r}$ = .26 and a 95 percent confidence interval of .25–.28 (Ellis 2006).[2] This told me that the estimate of the effect size observed in my individual study was within the likely range of values for the true effect size. I had seen the elephant!

But I am getting ahead of myself. You may be wondering, "What's all this talk about *d* and *r*?"

---

[2] I talk about how and why I conducted this meta-analysis—and the big mistake I made doing it—in Book 3, *Meta-Analysis Made Easy.*

Two families of effect size

Effect sizes come in many shapes and sizes. Some have familiar names like odds ratio and relative risk. Some double-up as test statistics (e.g., r, R^2), and others sound like planets from Star Trek (e.g., the Pillai-Bartlett V).

To be honest, I can't name all the effect sizes. But then, it's possible no one can. Kirk (2003) reckons there are at least 70 varieties but that number likely grows with each new statistical innovation.

Effect sizes are a bit like elements on the periodic table. There are some basic and well-known indexes at one end and some obscure and recently discovered indexes at the other.

The good news is that you don't need to know all the effect size indexes. All you really need to know is that most of them can be grouped into one of two families:

1. the d family, which includes indexes assessing the differences between groups
2. the r family, which includes measures of association

The *d* family: how different are these groups?

Are women drivers better than male drivers? Are right-handed batters more successful than lefties? Are those in the treatment group better off than those in the control group? Answers to these sorts of questions may be dichotomous (e.g., yes/no, pass/fail) or continuous (e.g., test scores) in nature.

When we compare groups on dichotomous variables, comparisons may be based on the probabilities of group members being classified into one of the two categories. Relevant effect sizes for this sort of comparison include the **odds ratio** and **relative risk**.

These two indexes are similar but different. Relative risk compares the *probability* of an outcome occurring in one group with the probability of it occurring in another, while the odds ratio compares the *odds* of an outcome occurring in one group with the odds of it occurring in another. If you know the difference between probabilities (p) and odds ($p/1 - p$), you know the difference between these two indexes.

When we compare groups on continuous variables the usual practice is to gauge the difference in the average or mean scores of each group. In theory, this is quite simple:

$$\frac{M_1 - M_2}{SD_{population}}$$

To calculate the difference between two groups we subtract the mean of one group from the mean of the other ($M_1 - M_2$) and divide the result by the standard deviation (SD) of the population from which the groups have been sampled. Easy peasy lemon squeezy!

The only tricky part in this calculation is figuring out the population standard deviation. Typically this number is unknown so we must rely on some approximate value instead. Since there are at least three ways to come up with that value, there are three ways to calculate the mean difference between two groups:

Cohen's d	Glass's Δ	Hedges' g
$\dfrac{M_1 - M_2}{SD_{pooled}}$	$\dfrac{M_1 - M_2}{SD_{control}}$	$\dfrac{M_1 - M_2}{SD*_{pooled}}$

Which is best? It depends.

When comparing groups a good way to proceed is to examine the standard deviations of each group. If they are about the same we can reasonably assume they are estimating a common population standard deviation. In this case we would pool the two SDs to calculate a **Cohen's *d*.** If they are not the same we could assume that the SD of the control group is closer to the true population SD and calculate a **Glass's Δ** or delta. And if the groups are dissimilar in size we could pool the weighted SD's and calculate a **Hedges' g.**

(If you're interested, equations for fiddling around with standard deviations are found in *The Essential Guide to Effect Sizes*. If you're not interested, but you have to do it anyway, just plug your numbers into an online calculator such as the one I'll tell you about below.)

The *r* family: how strong is this relationship?

How strong are the links between smoking and cancer, Facebook use and academic performance, kissing and Covid-19? These sorts of questions lead to effect sizes of the second kind, namely, measures of association linking two or more variables. Many of these measures are variations on the **correlation coefficient** (*r*), for instance, the **rank correlation coefficient**, the **point-biserial correlation coefficient**, *R* **squared**, **eta squared**, and so forth.

If you have done any sort of stats course, you will know about *r* and its derivatives. What you may not know is that r is one of the most popular measures of effect size.

There are dozens of effect size index and you don't need to know them all. However, you should have a passing familiarity with some of the more popular metrics, and these are listed in Table 2.

Table 2: Fifteen common effect size indexes

The *d* Family	The *r* Family

Groups compared on...
 (a) dichotomous outcomes
   - the risk difference (RD) in probabilities
   - the risk ratio or relative risk (RR)
   - the odds ratio (OR)
	(a) Correlation indexes
	   - the Pearson product moment correlation coefficient (r)
	   - Spearman's rho or the rank correlation coefficient (ρ or r_s)
	   - point-biserial correlation coefficient (r_{pb})
	   - the phi coefficient (φ)

(b) continuous outcomes
   - Cohen's *d*
   - Glass's Δ
      Hedges' *g*
	(b) Proportion of variance indexes
	   - the coefficient of determination (r^2)
	   - R squared, or the (uncorrected) coefficient of multiple determination (R^2)
	   - adjusted R squared ($_{adj}R^2$)
	   - Cohen's *f*
	   - eta squared or the (uncorrected) correlation ratio (η^2)

How to calculate an effect size

Often when I tell people about effect sizes, one of the first things they ask is, "What software do I need to calculate them?" That's a bit like saying, "What do I need to catch an animal?" It depends on the animal.

There is no one-size-fits-all program that will generate effect sizes for every situation, and you don't really need one. Effect size indexes in the d family can be calculated on the back of an envelope or in a spreadsheet. If you can subtract and divide you can calculate Glass's Δ. Admittedly, it gets a bit more complicated when you start fiddling around with the denominator, but most of the time you will be able to find an online calculator simply by googling the name of the desired index (e.g., "Cohen's d calculator" or "relative risk calculator").

Effect size indexes in the r-family are often generated automatically by statistical programs such as SPSS or STATA.[3]

---

[3] For a list of SPSS procedures that can be used to calculate 25 common effect size indexes, see Table 1.2 in *The Essential Guide to Effect Sizes* (Ellis 2010b).

Can you recommend an effect size calculator?

A few years ago I hired a programmer to build a webpage with seven of the most-used calculators all in one place. I gave her the formulas and she gave me a functional website that anyone can use. Figure 2 provides a screenshot.

Figure 2: Effect size calculators[4]

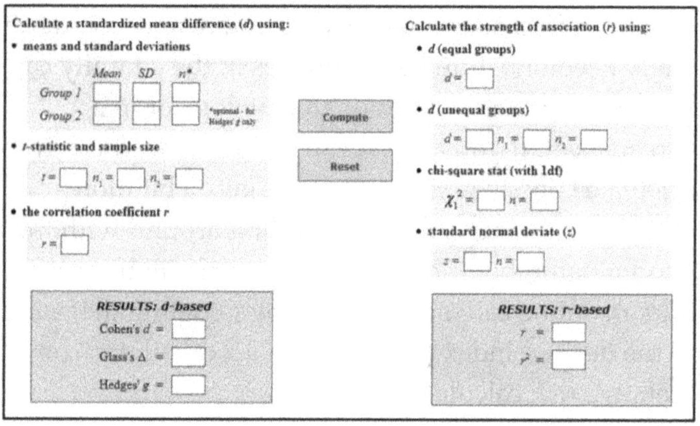

How does it work? Let's say you are comparing two groups and for each group you have the usual descriptive statistics (means and SDs). By plugging these four numbers into the boxes on the top-left of the page and then clicking the compute button in the

---

[4] Most of the resources mentioned in this book can be accessed from effectsizefaq.com/resources.

middle, you will automatically get an effect size expressed in terms of Cohen's d and Glass's Δ. And if you input the group sizes as well, you'll get a Hedges' g for good measure.

Or perhaps you want to calculate the effect size of a published study but the authors neglected to include descriptive statistics. Did they include a t-stat? Then enter that number along with the two group sizes and you'll get a d-based metric.

One neat thing about this app is that it will automatically convert your d to an r, just for fun. This means if you have multiple studies examining the same effect but reporting results in different metrics, you can convert their results to a common metric and compare them. Suddenly, without trying, you have become a meta-analyst!

Why are editors increasingly asking authors to report effect sizes?

Because the whole point of doing research is so that we may learn something about real world effects.

Until recently, the publishability of any study was largely determined by the results of statistical significance tests. Get a low p value and *voila!* Your hypothesis was supported and you had a story to tell.

But that was then and this is now.

Editors are increasingly coming to realize that p values tell us very little about the phenomena we study. True, they can signal the direction of an effect (positive, negative, or none at all). But they can't tell us how big the effect is. And if we can't say whether the effect is large or small, how can we draw meaningful conclusions? How can we interpret our result?

Let's say you're interested in the effect of sun-bathing on skin cancer. You read every study you can find on sun-bathing and skin cancer, you design a study to assess the link between sun-bathing and skin cancer, and you collect data on sun-bathing and skin cancer. But what happens next? Do you tell us how strong the relationship is? Not if you're among the 95 percent of researchers who subscribe to null hypothesis significance testing. No, you test a hypothesis no one is interested in, namely, the null hypothesis that sun-bathing has *no effect* on skin cancer. If all goes well, you reject that straw man. If the sign is in the expected direction, you'll conclude that, "Yes, there is an effect; sun-bathing has some effect on skin cancer."

And what have we learned?

Precisely nothing.

We already knew that sun bathing leads to skin cancer. (We've read the previous studies too.) What we really want to know is, how big is this effect and what does it mean? Should we change our sun bathing behavior? Should we stop sun-bathing? Your null hypothesis significance test can't answer these questions—it's not designed to. Consequently, your contribution to knowledge is close to zilch.

Editors understand this which is why they are now asking for more. Look at your data again. How big is the r (if you have one) or the d (ditto)? How do your estimates of the effect size compare with estimates obtained in other studies? Are the estimates converging on a common population effect size or are they diverging for predictable reasons? And what do your results mean for the average sun-bather?

After all, isn't this why you're doing the research in the first place—to save sun-bathers?

Which journals encourage the reporting of effect sizes?

Editors encourage effect size reporting two ways: (1) by explicitly asking authors to report effect sizes in their submission guidelines, or (2) by asking authors to interpret the substantive significance of their findings (which can only be done by examining effect sizes). Editors and editorial board members who deserve praise for promoting effect size reporting are listed in Table 3.

This may not be a particularly large list, but look at the journals on it. Some of them are among the best in their fields. They are the trend-setters. It is inevitable that this list will grow as reporting practices promulgated in the top-tier journals are adopted by others.

The journal I am submitting to says nothing about reporting effect sizes. Should I do it anyway?

Of course! How else will you interpret the substantive significance of your results without referring to your effect size estimates? (Remember, this is one of five compelling reasons mentioned at the start of this book for reporting effect sizes.)

Table 3: Editors who encourage effect size reporting

Journal	Editor
Academy of Management J.	Combs (2010), Rynes (2007)
Educational & Psychological Measurement	Thompson (1994)
J. of Applied Psychology	Campbell (1982), Murphy (1997), Zedeck (2003)
J. of Consulting & Clinical Psychology	Kendall (1997), La Greca (2005)
J. of Consumer Research	Iacobucci (2005)
J. of Counseling and Development	Thompson (2002)
J. of Educational Psychology	JEP (2003)
J. of Experimental Psychology	Melton (1962)
J. of Family Psychology	Levant (1992)
J. of Int. Business Studies	Shaver (2006)
J. of Learning Disabilities	Hresko (2000)
J. of Rehabilitation	Lustig and Strauser (2004)
Personnel Psychology	Campion (1993)
Research in the Schools	McLean and Kaufman (2000)

Researchers who focus on the results of statistical significance tests at the expense of effect sizes are under-selling their results. They are essentially throwing away hard-earned data and settling for contributions that are less than what they really have to offer.

They are like the proverbial prosecutor trying to win his case without referring to the evidence.

It is true that many journals presently do not require the reporting of effect sizes. Scan the author guidelines for some journals and you won't even find the phrase "effect size." But you can bet your house that this will change over time, and that a growing number of disciplines will follow the lead of psychology because effect size reporting is the right and smart thing to do.

It is a habit we should have adopted 40 years ago.

And although many editors may have no explicit policy on effect size reporting, you may encounter reviewers who do. I have served on seven editorial review boards and reviewed countless papers and I always insist on the reporting of effect sizes. I am utterly pedantic about it. This is not about me promoting a pet statistical technique; I simply want to see the evidence that authors have collected. So do others.

A paper that doesn't report effect sizes is like a whodunit novel without the final chapter or a riddle without a punch line. It is unfinished. By coaching authors through the review process I have helped many tease out results and contributions that were far more meaningful than what they thought they had.

Why haven't I heard about effect sizes before?

The simple answer is you are probably not a psychologist.

Methodological innovations have to come from somewhere and in the social sciences, many originate in the field of psychology. Read any top psychology journal and you may be surprised at the emphasis given to methodology and statistical innovation. Evidently, there is something about the study of psychology that appeals to statisticians. Or maybe it's the other way around.

Effect sizes may be new to you but Jacob Cohen, formerly of NYU's psychology department, was writing brilliant little papers about them 60 years ago (Cohen 1962). In the 1970s, Gene Glass and Mary Lee Smith collected effect sizes in their pioneering meta-analysis of psychotherapy treatments (Glass 1976, Smith and Glass 1977).

By the 1990s Wilkinson and the Taskforce on Statistical Inference, in their recommendations to the American Psychological Association, were arguing that the reporting and interpretation of effect sizes is "essential to good research" (1999: 599). So effect sizes have been around for some time.

In my own discipline, international business, very few researchers are in the habit of reporting and interpreting effect sizes. This may be the case with your discipline as well.

But if history has taught us anything, it's that psychology is the Silicon Valley of statistical reform. Innovations and practices developed there are often adopted later in other social science disciplines. After all, these are the guys who wrote the manual most of us follow when submitting our papers for publication. I am referring to the *Publication Manual of the American Psychological Association*, which says this:

> For the reader to appreciate the magnitude or importance of a study's findings, it is almost always necessary to include some measure of effect size in the Results Section. (APA 2010: 34)

If psychologists are big believers in effect size reporting, odds are this practice will become commonplace in other disciplines. So get in ahead of the pack and develop the habit of reporting and interpreting effect sizes.

Why wasn't I taught effect sizes in Research Methods 101?

Good question! The most likely answer is that your teacher was never taught about effect sizes and you can't teach what you haven't learned.

As I mentioned, I taught Research Methods to Ph.D. students for 15 years and for part of that time I was ignorant of effect sizes. It wasn't until I began learning about meta-analysis that I realized the estimation of effect sizes is a fundamental, if oft-ignored, goal of all research. Hopefully your teachers were better-informed than me, but odds are they weren't.

Why does my research methods textbook have no entry for "effect size"?

Because it's out of date. It's a dinosaur, a relic of a bygone age.

As a methods teacher I have accumulated a substantial library of methods books. Prior to writing *The Essential Guide to Effect Sizes*, I scanned all of these books plus dozens more in the library to see if they said *anything* about effect sizes. I discovered that close to 90 percent of textbooks said nothing at all, and the few that did mention effect sizes usually did so only in passing (e.g., with reference to meta-analysis).

My library tour sadly confirmed the perception that many textbooks are 20–30 years behind the game. On the one hand, we have the editors of prestigious journals and the presidents of academic societies calling for the reporting of effect sizes; on the other, we have methods texts and methods classes that are doing nothing in response to those calls. It was this disconnect that prompted me to write the book you are now reading.

A typical methods text will show you how a hundred different ways to assess the statistical significance of a test, but it won't show you how to interpret the substantive significance of your results. It will talk about p values but say next to nothing about effect sizes.

This will change.

As the number of journal editors insisting on effect size reporting continues to grow, the number researchers learning how to report them will also grow. Some will write books about it. My guess is that in 10–20 years' time, effect sizes will be covered in the majority of methods texts.

You read it here first.

Intermission

In Part A our focus was on reporting estimates of the effect size. One of the reasons we do this is so that we can draw conclusions about real world effects.

If the question in Part A was, "how big is it?" the question we now turn to in Part B is, "what does it mean and to whom?"

How to answer the most important question you'll ever be asked in a research presentation

"So what?"

"Why did you do this study?"

"What impact does this have for the real world?"

These questions provoke nervous smiles and evasive answers, but they are legitimate questions that deserve legitimate answers. They certainly deserve answers better than these:

"This study contributes to our understanding of XYZ." *Whoop-de-doo.*

"The results shed light on the relationship between X and Y." *Yawn. Somebody fetch me a pillow.*

"The findings show that Y is affected by X." *We probably could've guessed that without doing a study. Why not tell us how big the effect is and what it means.*

"The results provide further evidence of a link between X and Y." *After three years of careful study that's it?! You're telling us you discovered something we already knew?*

It's responses like these that give researchers a bad name.

Failing to communicate the real world significance of our work reinforces the public's perception that academics are no earthly good, that we teach because we can't do, and that we inhabit little bubbles of irrelevance.

A colleague of mine once compared researchers to medieval alchemists. "Instead of turning base metals into gold, we're turning taxpayer's money into conference papers." Sadly, there is a measure of truth behind this cynical observation.

Researchers occupy a privileged position in society. We exist at the pleasure of the taxpayer or benefactor. So when society asks the hard "so what?" questions, it behooves us to offer intelligent answers. The problem is that most of us don't know how to answer these questions in any meaningful way. We have never been taught how. We know how to collect and analyze data but the bit that comes after that remains a mystery.

How do most researchers draw conclusions from their studies?

Since most of us have not been taught to report effect sizes, it follows that most of us don't know how to interpret them. And if we're not interpreting effect sizes, what are we interpreting instead? On what basis are we drawing conclusions from our studies?

Many researchers draw conclusions by looking at the results of statistical significance tests. They follow what we might call a p-based logic of ascribing meaning. This p-based logic runs like this:

- if $p > .10$, then the test result is interpreted as providing no support for the hypothesis
- if $.05 < p < .10$, the result is interpreted as providing marginal support
- if $p < .05$, the result is interpreted as supporting the hypothesis

I have seen some studies that go even further and interpret a result of $p < .01$ or $.001$ as "strong support" or "strong confirmation" or "strong evidence" for whatever they are looking for (see Figure 3).

It's a common practice to interpret the substantive significance of a test result by looking at its statistical significance, but it's bad science.

Figure 3: The relationship between *p*-values and researcher happiness

Statistical significance tests have their uses—they are useful for managing the risk of mistaking random sampling variation for genuine effects—but we cannot use them to draw substantive conclusions about the effects we are studying. Why not? A story will help explain…

What is the difference between and effect size and a *p* value?

Two groups of sports fans argued over who knew more about wrestling. Rednecks argued that slack-jawed yokels "don't know the first thang 'bout rassling," while the SJY's replied that "yer average redneck cain't tell diff'rence 'tween the dub-dub-F and the dub-dub-E."

The bickering continued until both groups decided to settle the matter with a quiz about wrestling trivia. To keep things fair and above board, each group recruited an independent researcher to administer the test.

Since neither group trusted the other, the same test was done twice, one after the other. In each test, rednecks and SJYs were asked a set of questions about wrestling. To no one's surprise, the results of both studies, in terms of test scores and standard deviations, turned out to be exactly the same (see Table 4).

Although both studies found that rednecks scored higher than SJYs, the results from Study 2 were not statistically significant (i.e., $p > .05$). This led the author of Study 2 to conclude that there was no statistical difference between the groups in terms of their knowledge of wrestling trivia.

However, the author of Study 1 came to a different conclusion. She noted that the 25–point difference in mean test scores was substantial in size being just less than one standard deviation. This author concluded that rednecks are substantially more knowledgeable than SJYs when it comes to wrestling trivia.

Table 4: Test scores for knowledge of wrestling trivia

	Mean	SD	N	t	p	Cohen's d
Study 1						
Rednecks	75	30	25	1.84	< .05	0.83
SJYs	50	30	25			
Study 2						
Rednecks	75	30	20	1.65	> .05	0.83
SJYs	50	30	20			

The author of Study 1 said there was a big difference between the groups, while the author of Study 2 said there was no difference. How could two studies with identical methods relying on identical samples to estimate identical effect sizes lead to such different conclusions?

The answer has to do with the misuse of statistical significance testing. When interpreting the results of their study, the author of Study 2 ignored the estimate of the effect size and focused on the p value. He incorrectly interpreted a statistically nonsignificant result as indicating no effect. However, a nonsignificant result is more accurately interpreted as an *inconclusive* result. There might be no effect, or there might be an effect but the study lacked the statistical power to detect it. In this case we have good reason to lean towards the latter conclusion.

Why so?

Take another look in the numbers in Table 4 paying particular attention to the descriptive stats. A 25 point difference between the group means seems big, but in truth it's meaningless unless we know something about the standard deviation or the spread of the results. The d (0.83) in the far right column tells us that the difference between the groups is equivalent to five-sixths of a standard deviation. That is a big difference in anyone's language. It tells us that rednecks are considerably smarter than SJYs.

The author of Study 1 saw this whopper of a difference but the author of Study 2 missed it. How?

He was distracted by his p value.

This begs the question, if the effect was so big, how come the statistical test didn't bear fruit in Study 2? And how come it did in Study 1? Why did these identical studies generate different p values?

The reason is that after the first study, ten participants thought it was stupid to take the same test again so they went home. Hence the conclusions for Study 2 were drawn from a smaller pooled sample (40 people instead of 50) and the consequent drain on statistical power meant that a genuine effect went undetected. This leads us to one of the most important questions in this book...

Why can't we draw substantive conclusions from p values?

Because p values are affected by several factors, only one of which is the size of the underlying effect. Here's an equation to illustrate this point:

statistical significance = effect size x sample size

Statistical significance is inversely proportional to the p value of a test result. A high p means the result is not statistically significant and vice versa. What the equation above tells us is that, other things being equal, the bigger the effect the smaller the p. In other words, the bigger the thing you are trying to find, the easier it is to find it—the more likely your results will be statistically significant. So a small p could indicate a large effect size, but not necessarily.

Now look at the other side of that equation. All things being equal, the bigger the sample the smaller the p. In other words, the wider your net, the more likely you'll catch something, even if the thing you're fishing for is tiny. Conversely, the smaller the sample the bigger the p. As samples shrink it becomes harder to achieve statistical significance even when large effects are being observed.

In the wrestling example, the effect size was identical in both studies but the sample size was smaller for study 2. (Ten people went home, remember?) As N went down, p went up. It had to—sample size and statistical significance are directly related. This is why the test results differed between the studies.

I cover these issues in my MadMethods book *Statistical Power Trip*. All you need to know here is that you should never judge the substantive significance of a result by looking at a p value. P values are confounded indexes. They are affected by several variables only one of which is the effect size.

To draw any sort of substantive conclusion from a result, you need to look directly at the estimate of the effect size. This could be a d-equivalent variable if you are comparing groups, or some variation of r if you are examining the strength of association. But unless you know what *It* is and how big *It* is, then you won't be able to say anything meaningful about *It*.

Capiche?

"I got a significant result"—what's wrong with this statement?

In a typical methods class, students are taught to assess the statistical significance of their results. This is a useful skill but it can lead to meaningless claims like the one above. My students quickly learned never to say things like that.

"Professor, I got a significant result!"

"Grrrrrr!"

What's the problem? The problem is the word significant requires qualification. What type of significance are we talking about? Because there is more than one:

-   statistical significance = the result exceeds certain statistical criteria
-   practical or substantive significance = the result is meaningful in the real world

Think of it this way: Only researchers and statisticians understand the first kind of significance, while the second kind makes sense to real people like plumbers, painters, and publicans. Since we are attempting to do research that matters, we need to be as familiar with the latter as the former.

Since there are at two kinds of significance, there are four possible outcomes for any research result. A result can be statistically significant and practically meaningless, vice versa, neither, or both. To say, "I got a significant result," begs the question, "What sort of significance are we talking about?"

Usually, it's the wrong sort.

Don't get me wrong, statistical significance is nice to have. But at the end of the day what really matters is substantive significance. To see how well you understand this, consider the following research scenario, which is adapted from Kirk (1996):

> You are testing a new drug which you hope will improve the IQ of Alzheimer's patients. You administer the drug to a test group and a placebo to a control group. After some time you test both groups and find...

> Outcome 1   The treatment group now has an average IQ 13 points higher than the control group—an appreciable difference. However, the p value is high (.14) making the result statistically nonsignificant.

Outcome 2   The difference between the groups
is small, just 2 IQ points, but the p
value is low (0.04) making the
result statistically significant.

Which outcome do you prefer? Review the two
outcomes again and take a moment to decide
which one you would rather see.

Have you made your choice? Okay. This is not a trick
question. Outcome 1 is clearly better. A thirteen point
improvement is better than a two point improvement.
But if you hesitated before choosing this outcome, or
worse, you chose Outcome 2, then that should tell
you something.

Perhaps you dismissed the results of Outcome 1 as a
fluke. After all, the results are statistically nonsignificant. If so, then you risk discarding a potentially
brilliant cure.

Or perhaps you got excited about the statistically
significant result of Outcome 2. If so, you risk di-
recting future research down a dead end. You could
spend the next five to ten years of your career in-
vested in a drug that probably doesn't work.

Look again at the effect sizes (the change in IQ) and
make a judgment without regard for the p value.
Wouldn't you agree that a thirteen point gain is a

bigger and intrinsically more interesting result than a two point gain? Outcome 2 gave us a statistically significant result, but Outcome 1 gave us a result of substantive significance.

What would I do with these two outcomes? In the case of Outcome 1, I would be encouraged to do a bigger study. We may be on to a winner and chances are the low p value is the result of an underpowered research design. In the case of Outcome 2, I would be tempted to abandon the drug and move on to other things. It seems to be a dud.

Anyway, we were talking about the different meanings of significance.

In research it is possible, and unfortunately quite common, for a result to be statistically significant yet trivial. It is also possible for a result to be statistically nonsignificant yet meaningful.

However, researchers rarely distinguish between these two types of significance. What usually happens is that results which are found to be statistically significant are interpreted as if they were practically meaningful. This happens when a researcher interprets a statistically significant result as "significant" or "highly significant."

Do researchers really get confused about this significance stuff?

I surveyed six years' worth of research in a leading business journal to assess the extent to which researchers in my field are in the habit of reporting and interpreting effect sizes. My survey covered 204 independent studies reported in 189 separate articles (see Ellis 2010a).

In many of the studies I read, effect sizes were reported unintentionally. This occurred whenever authors reported test statistics that happen to double as effect size indicators (e.g., r, R^2, η^2). However, very few studies mentioned effect sizes explicitly. Consequently, it was no great surprise to find authors drawing conclusions that, frankly, were meaningless.

Some authors mentioned that their models "performed well." *Performed well with respect to what?* Others observed that their combination of predictors generated R^2s (or an increase in R^2s) that were "respectable" or "remarkable." *Respectable or remarkable in comparison with what?* Without a frame of reference, claims like these are meaningless.

Here are some other examples of meaningless conclusions that I came across:

- In one study statistical significance tests revealed that X had a positive influence on Y, "providing strong confirmation of (the effect)." *They provided no such thing. Statistical significance is affected by multiple factors, only one of which is the effect size.*

- "Test results provide strong evidence that Y ($p < 0.01$) is a function of X." *I don't doubt that there is evidence of a link in your study but that low p reveals nothing about the strength of such a link. Chances are you just had a really large sample.*

- "Overall the empirical model performs well: it is highly significant, and records a pseudo-R^2 of 0.37, which is respectable for logit models." *This would be funny if it wasn't so cringeworthy. It's like there's this country club for respectable logit models. Models which achieve lower R-squareds aren't welcome. They can go hang out in a B-grade journal with the other riff-raff.*

- One author observed a "remarkable jump" in R^2. *Goody! Maybe they'll let him into that exclusive club for respectable logits.*

- "All the coefficients have the hypothesized sign and are significant." *[Insert anguished sounds of frustration and hair-pulling here.] I am happy for you that the signs are as expected; I am not happy that you are blurring the lines between substantive and*

64

statistical significance. Take care, you're confusing the children! Ph.D. students are reading this.

Equally meaningless was the claim that a test statistic was bigger or more impressive than a result obtained in an earlier study. If separate studies are estimating the same population effect then results should be celebrated for converging, rather than diverging. If they are estimating different effects then there is little to be gained by comparing them.

Reading these studies, it soon became clear that the majority of international business researchers do not report nor interpret their estimates of effect size. One notable exception was Baggs and Brander's (2006, p.207) attempt to convey in plain English the "economic significance" of the effects of trade liberalization in Canada:

> The effect of a large import tariff reduction reduces profit by $146,000 for an average firm. At this rate, many firms protected by initially large tariffs would have profits reduced to zero over the phase-in period.

This is a useful conclusion for it conveys information about the size of an effect in language that is meaningful to non-specialists and uncomplicated by subsidiary issues of statistical significance.

Regrettably, conclusions as clear as this were hard to find.

My survey results are not unusual. The common finding of similar surveys in other disciplines is that most authors make no attempt to interpret the practical or real world significance of their research results (see, for example, Andersen *et al.*, 2007; Kieffer *et al.*, 2001; McCloskey and Ziliak 1996).

Even scholars publishing in top-tier journals routinely confuse statistical with practical significance. In their review of 137 papers published in the *American Economic Review*, Ziliak and McCloskey (2004) found that 82 percent of authors mistook statistical significance for economic significance.

Eighty-two percent!

Cohen (1994: 1001) drew a similar conclusion after observing his colleagues' habits in the field of psychology.

> All psychologists know that *statistically significant* does not mean plain English significant, but if one reads the literature, one often discovers a finding reported in the Results section studded with asterisks implicitly becomes in the Discussion section highly significant, or very highly significant, important, big!

I've got an effect size—now what?

Interpret it. Use your own informed judgment to tell us what it means.

In the Alzheimer's example, I got excited about the prospect of a thirteen point gain in IQ. But since I have no experience working with Alzheimer's patients I don't really know how meaningful a thirteen point gain is. So let me ask you what you think.

Imagine that someone you care about is suffering from advanced Alzheimer's. If a thirteen point gain in IQ meant they could now remember your name and face, would you judge that to be a "significant" improvement? You probably would.

Okay, what about a gain that was only half as big, say, six IQ points? Still significant? It's harder to say but only you can make this judgment. There's no book you can look up to decide whether a six point improvement is meaningful. It's meaningful if you say it is; it's not if you say it isn't.

Here's the point: effects mean different things to different people. What is a big deal to you may not be a big deal to me and vice versa. The interpretation of effect sizes inevitably involves a value judgment and this makes researchers uncomfortable. We prefer the cold distance of objectivity to the warm-fuzzies of subjective interpretation. We would rather be Mr. Spock than Captain Kirk.

But if you don't interpret your own findings, who will?

> No one is in a better position than the researcher who collected and analyzed the data to decide whether the effects are trivial or not. It is a curious anomaly that researchers are trusted to make a variety of complex decisions in the design and execution of an experiment, but in the name of objectivity they are not expected to nor even encouraged to decide whether the effects are practically significant. (Kirk 2001:214)

Failing to interpret your study's findings is like quitting a marathon a quarter mile short of the finish line. You've done all the work—you've designed and executed a study—now tell us what you found and what it means.

As we have seen, the wrong way to do this is to look at p values. The right way is to look at the effect size. Is it big or small? In comparison with what? Is it big enough to be meaningful? How does it compare with what others have found?

How do I interpret my results?

Imagine your doctor tells you this:

> Research shows that people with your body-mass index and sedentary lifestyle score on average two points lower on a cardiac risk assessment test in comparison with active people with a healthy body weight.

Would these words prompt you to make drastic changes to your lifestyle? Probably not. Not because the effect is trivial but because you have no way of interpreting its meaning. What does "two points lower" mean? Is two points a big deal? Should you be worried? Being unfamiliar with the scale, you are unable to draw any conclusion.

Now imagine your doctor says this instead:

> Research shows that people with your body-mass index and sedentary lifestyle are four times as likely to suffer a serious heart attack within 10 years in comparison with active people with a normal body weight.

Now the doctor has your full attention. This time you're sitting on the edge of your seat gripped with a resolve to lose weight and start exercising again. Hearing about the research in terms which are familiar to you, you are better able to extract their meaning and draw conclusions.

When it comes to interpreting effects, context matters. Effect sizes are meaningless unless they can be contextualized against some frame of reference, such as a well-known scale or prior findings.

Can you give us an example of how to interpret an effect size?

Earlier I mentioned how I found a relationship between market orientation and business performance equivalent to $r = 0.25$. That's the effect size, but what does it mean? What is the practical significance of this result? How do we interpret it?

A statistician would be tempted to express this result in terms of the proportion of shared variance. In other words, they'll square it (.25 x .25) and conclude that 6¼ percent of the total variance is shared between the two variables. Even if you don't know what that means, it sounds small—just 6¼ percent. That sounds like market orientation does not have much of an effect on performance at all.

That's one conclusion; here's another.

Business performance is affected by a thousand different factors. Some factors, like product design, branding, etc., are controllable, while many other factors, like the cost of materials, the exchange rate, the weather, pandemics, etc., are uncontrollable. It is rare for any single factor to account for a substantial proportion of business performance—there are just too many variables at play. So to find a single factor, market orientation, that accounts for 6¼ percent is noteworthy.

The world of business is complex. The average size of any effect in business is very low, just $r = 0.06$ (Ellis 2010a). Finding an effect of size $r = 0.25$ is like finding a whale in a fish tank. It stands out.

When it comes to interpreting results, context matters. In absolute terms, market orientation has a smallish effect on performance. But compared to every other factor, it has a relatively big effect. Knowing and responding to customers better than rivals is the gas pedal of business. Learning how to do this well is one thing managers and business owners can do to maximize their performance.

Allow me to recap in case you missed my point. I *reported* a smallish effect size then I *interpreted* it by comparing it with other factors affecting performance. Most effects in business are tiny; my one was bigger than tiny so it stands out. And

71

because performance affects the life and death of any business, any effect that is bigger than the rest is likely to matter a great deal. See? By contextualizing my finding against other business effects, I gave meaning to my result.

In the Baggs and Brander (2006) study, the authors said that the effect of a large tariff reduction would be to reduce profit by $146,000 for an average firm. By conveying the effect size in terms of dollars and cents, instead of, say, p values, model fits, or changes in R^2s, these authors deliver a startlingly clear interpretation of the effect size. If you are the manager of an average firm, you will be left with an excellent idea of what the proposed tariff reduction means for your business.

It's small, but is it important?

Effect sizes are like animals; the big ones are few in number (like elephants) while the little ones are abundant (like ants). Often your research will reveal an effect which is tiny. That doesn't mean it is trivial. Some of the most interesting effects in science are small.

In the right context, small effects may be big enough to be meaningful. Presidential elections are sometimes decided on the smallest of margins. Gold medals and Olympic glory go to those who win by hundredths of a second. Just as small sparks start big fires, small effects are substantively significant when they trigger large outcomes.

Small effects can also be important if they accumulate into larger effects, such as lives saved. Consider a drug that reduces the risk of heart attacks by four percent for at-risk people. That doesn't sound like a big effect but in a large country such as the United States, this figure translates into 6,500 saved lives every year. (The drug is propranolol if you're wondering (Kolata 1981).)

Smoking gives us another example of the cumulative significance of small effects. Smokers like to argue that a single cigarette does little damage. "Just one can't hurt." In fact, scientists have calculated that a smoked cigarette will shorten your life by about eleven minutes. If you are regular smoker, those minutes add up fast. Smoke a daily packet of 20 cigarettes and you will shorten your life by a day for every week that you smoke (BBC 1999). Ouch!

The accumulation of small effects into big outcomes is often seen in sports. Consider "Abelson's Paradox" which describes how trivial effects can accumulate into meaningful effects over time. It is based on research Abelson (1985) did into the effects of batting skill on individual batting performance in baseball. Abelson found that batting skill has a pitifully small on individual performance. Nevertheless, skilled batters win games because they bat more than once per game and the miniscule effects of skill cumulate.

The challenge of interpretation

We have seen that the importance of an effect is determined by its context. If you can show what the effect means in plain language, you can speak directly to its meaning. But what if you can't?

Many phenomena in the social sciences can only be observed indirectly. For instance, to assess self-esteem, trust, or satisfaction levels, you might administer a questionnaire consisting of five- or seven-point scales. You know the drill. Respondents circle numbers that best describe their response where one means "strong disagree" and seven means "strong agree." It's simple to administer, but what do you do with the results? How do you translate circled numbers or mean values into meaningful metrics?

Arbitrary scales are useful for gauging effect sizes but they make interpretation problematic. You may find that "the treated group scored 3.5 points higher on average than the untreated group," but what does that mean to the person in the street? Did the treatment work? Do the benefits outweigh the costs?

In many cases, there will be no easy answers to these sorts of questions. But if you are unable to ground your arbitrary scale against a meaningful frame of reference, you may have no way of drawing a meaningful conclusion.

Fear not. All is not lost. Jacob Cohen has come to the rescue...

Cohen's effect size thresholds

As a last resort, one way to interpret a result is to refer to conventions governing effect size. The best known of these are the thresholds proposed by Cohen (1988) in his authoritative *Statistical Power Analysis for the Behavioral Sciences*. Table 5 summarizes Cohen's criteria for five effect sizes.

TABLE 5: Cohen's effect size benchmarks

Effect size	Effect size classes		
	Small	Medium	Large
d, Δ, g	.20	.50	.80
r	.10	.30	.50
r^2	.01	.09	.25

Source: Cohen (1988)

How does it work? Say you are comparing groups and you find the difference between the groups is equivalent to $d = 0.26$. According to Cohen's logic, this would qualify as a small effect, meaning, it exceeds the 0.2 cut-off for effects of this type. In our earlier example of wrestling knowledge, the difference between rednecks and SJYs was equivalent to $d = 0.83$. According to Cohen's metric, this would qualify as a large effect as it exceeds the 0.8 cut-off for d-based metrics.

The appeal of Cohen's effect size criteria is they are convenient. You just plug in your effect size and get a ready-made interpretation.

How did Cohen come up with these thresholds?

I'm glad you asked, because there's an interesting story behind them.

In deciding the thresholds for the different effect sizes, Cohen began by defining a medium effect as one "visible to the naked eye of the careful observer" (Cohen 1992: 156). His example? The difference in height between 14 and 18 year old girls, which is about one inch (Cohen 1988: 26).

Having defined a medium-sized effect, it was a straightforward matter to define small and large effects. Cohen defined a small effect as equivalent to the height difference between 15 and 16 year old girls, which is about half an inch. A large effect was defined as one that is as far above a medium effect as a small one is below it. In this case, a large effect is equivalent to the height difference between 13 and 18 year old girls, which is just over an inch and a half.

Why did Cohen decide to look at teenage girls when deciding on these metrics? I have no idea. It's a mystery. But at least his method sounds more fun than the one adopted by Karl Pearson.

Pearson (1905) devised effect size thresholds for the correlation metric r by considering the relationship between a man's left and right thigh bones (highly correlated); the relationship between the height of fathers and their sons (considerably correlated); and the relationship between a woman's height and her pulling strength (low correlation)!

Why should we hesitate to use Cohen's thresholds?

Cohen's effect size thresholds are not without controversy. Noted scholars such as Gene Glass have argued that the classification of effects into t-shirt sizes of small, medium and large hinders real interpretation (Glass *et al.*, 1981). This is a valid point.

Earlier I mocked the convention of drawing conclusions from different p values. We might just as easily mock the convention of drawing conclusions from Cohen's thresholds. I agree with Shaver (1993: 303) who said, "Substituting sanctified effect size conventions for the sanctified .05 level of statistical significance is not progress."

To be fair, Cohen knew this when he published his thresholds. He said his conventions were devised "with much diffidence, qualifications, and invitations not to employ them if possible" (1988: 532).

The proper way to view Cohen's thresholds is as an interpretation tool of last resort. You might use them when you have no other basis for drawing meaning from your results. The fact that they are used at all — given that they have no raison d'être beyond Cohen's study of teenage girls — speaks volumes about the inherent difficulties of assessing the substantive significance of our results. Interpretation is essential but often difficult.

The good news is this issue is attracting attention from a growing number of scholars. In recent years a number of helpful guidelines have emerged to assist authors with the interpretation challenge. If you are interested, check out the work by Blanton and Jaccard (2006), Cumming and Finch (2005), Hoetker (2007), and Shaver (2008).

We'll finish this book with something fun.

The delightfully whimsical yet sort of serious Result Whacker

A few years ago I was given some grant money to develop the effect size calculators I mentioned in Part A. When I was done I had some money left over, which is criminal when dealing with bureaucratic largesse. Rather than admit my budgeting weaknesses, I gave the left-over money to a programmer with instructions to develop something called the Result Whacker (see Figure 4).

The Result Whacker is a bit of fun that serves a serious purpose. The fun part is plugging your effect size (either a d- or r-equivalent) into the relevant box, then pressing "Whack." If you have entered a large effect size, say $d = 2$ or $r = 1$, the puck flies up the tower and hits the bell. Alternatively, if your effect size is pitifully small, the puck barely moves. It's hilarious.

Well, it is if you're caffeinated to the gills after crunching numbers for ten hours straight.

Figure 4: The Result Whacker[5]

The Result Whacker is fun, but it serves an educational purpose. First, the labels on the right side of the Result Whacker correspond to Cohen's effect size conventions. If you enter $d = 0.2$, the puck will just make it to "small." But if you enter 0.1999999, the puck won't cross the threshold. Add as many 9s as you like, it's not going to get there.

So one purpose of the Whacker is to let people know that, rightly or wrongly, there are conventions out there which may be used for interpreting effects of different size.

---

[5] Source: bit.ly/RO9wj4

The second purpose of the Whacker is to make you think. After playing with the Whacker for a few minutes you begin to wonder, "Isn't this all a bit silly? Can't we do better than mindlessly plugging in numbers and whacking out a ready-made interpretation? Aren't we better than this?"

Hopefully we are.

In this regard the Result Whacker is a conversation starter, a stimulus to real interpretation.

I suppose the Result Whacker should come with a health warning. Use it without thinking and you are in just as much danger of mindless interpretation as those who draw substantive conclusions from the results of statistical significance tests.

The main takeaway from this book

In this book we have learned that most researchers fail to distinguish between the statistical- and substantive significance of their results. Consequently, most are unable to provide meaningful responses to the "so what?" question. In response, we have looked at different ways for extracting meaning from our results. We have also identified some of the pioneering journals that are now insisting on effect size reporting, and we have learned how to calculate effect sizes in a variety of metrics. If I was to distill the most important lesson of this book, it would be this: Report and interpret effect size estimates.

I said at the start that this was a book for hammer-whackers, but really there's only so much you can learn from whacking things. Real researchers *think*. They ponder and ruminate and deliberate. They entertain alternative plausible explanations and they extrapolate meaning by fitting their effect size estimates into meaningful contexts. Finally, they convey the import of their results in language that anyone can understand.

These are exciting times for researchers who believe their work can and should be of value to society. By conducting research that matters and presenting results that make sense, good researchers can change the world.

Author's note

If you enjoyed *Effect Size Matters*, would you mind posting a short customer review on Amazon? Doing so will help others find this book.

Thank you!

Appendix: Ten great quotes from dead researchers

"Research is the process of going up alleys to see if they are blind."

> — Marston Bates (1906–1974)
> American zoologist and author of books on ecology

"Somewhere, something incredible is waiting to be known."

> — Carl Sagan (1934–1996)
> American astronomer and science communicator

"Research is formalized curiosity. It is poking and prying with a purpose."

> — Zora Neale Hurston (1891–1960)
> American anthropologist and folklorist

"Basic research is when I am doing what I don't know what I am doing."

> — Werner von Braun (1912–1977)
> German scientist and designer of the
> Saturn V launch vehicle

"If we knew what we were doing it wouldn't be research."

> — Albert Einstein (1879–1955)
> the father of modern physics

"Research is to see what everybody else has seen, and to think what nobody else has thought"
> — Albert Szent-Györgyi (1893–1986)
> Hungarian biochemist who discovered vitamin C

"By seeking and blundering we learn."
> — Johann Wolfgang von Goethe (1749–1832)
> German science philosopher and rock collector

"What is research, but a blind date with knowledge?"
> — William J. Henry (1774–1836)
> British chemist who formulated Henry's Law

"Research serves to make building stones out of stumbling blocks."
> — Arthur D. Little (1863–1935)
> American chemist who discovered acetate

"Study hard what interests you the most in the most undisciplined, irreverent and original manner possible."
> — Richard Feynman (1918–1988)
> American theoretical physicist
> who helped develop the atom bomb

References

Abelson, R.P. (1985), "A variance explanation paradox: When a little is a lot," *Psychological Bulletin*, 97(1): 129–133.

Andersen, M.B., P. McCullagh, and G.J. Wilson (2007), "But what do the numbers really tell us? Arbitrary metrics and effect size reporting in sport psychology research," *Journal of Sport and Exercise Psychology*, 29(5): 664–672.

APA (2010), *Publication Manual of the American Psychological Association, 6th Edition.* Washington DC: American Psychological Association.

Baggs, J. and J.A. Brander (2006), "Trade liberalization, profitability, and financial leverage," *Journal of International Business Studies.* 37(2): 196–211.

BBC (1999), "Cigarettes cut life by 11 minutes," *BBC News,* website:
http://news.bbc.co.uk/2/hi/health/583722.stm

Blanton, H. and J. Jaccard (2006), "Arbitrary metrics in psychology," *American Psychologist*, 61(1): 27–41.

Campbell, J.P. (1982), "Editorial: Some remarks from the outgoing editor," *Journal of Applied Psychology*, 67(6): 691–700.

Campion, M.A. (1993), "Article review checklist: A criterion checklist for reviewing research articles in applied psychology," *Personnel Psychology*, 46(3): 705–718.

Cohen, J. (1962), "The statistical power of abnormal-social psychological research: A review," *Journal of Abnormal and Social Psychology*, 65(3): 145–153.

Cohen, J. (1988), *Statistical Power for the Behavioral Analysis, 2nd Edition*. Hillsdale: Lawrence Erlbaum.

Cohen, J. (1992), "A power primer," *Psychological Bulletin*, 112(1): 155–159.

Cohen, J. (1994), "The earth is round ($p<.05$)," *American Psychologist*, 49(12), 997–1003.

Combs, J.G. (2010), "Big samples and small effects: Let's not trade relevance and rigor for power," *Academy of Management Journal*. 53(1): 9–13.

Cumming, G. and S. Finch (2005), "Inference by eye: Confidence intervals and how to read pictures of data," *American Psychologist*, 60(2): 170–180.

Ellis, P.D. (2006), "Market orientation and performance: A meta-analysis and cross-national comparisons," *Journal of Management Studies*, 43(5): 1089–1107.

Ellis, P.D. (2007), "Distance, dependence and diversity of markets: Effects on market orientation," *Journal of International Business Studies*, 38(3): 374–386.

Ellis, P.D., (2010a) "Effect sizes and the interpretation of research results in international business," *Journal of International Business Studies*, 41(9): 1581–1588.

Ellis, P.D. (2010b), *The Essential Guide to Effect Sizes: An Introduction to Statistical Power, Meta-Analysis and the Interpretation of Research Results*. Cambridge University Press.

Glass, G. (1976), "Primary, secondary, and meta-analysis of research," *Educational Researcher* 5: 3–8.

Glass, G.V., B. McGaw, and M.L. Smith (1981), *Meta-Analysis in Social Research.* Sage: Beverly Hills.

Hoetker, G. (2007), The use of logit and probit models in strategic management research: Critical issues, *Strategic Management Journal,* 28: 331–343.

Hresko, W. (2000), "Editorial policy," *Journal of Learning Disabilities,* 33, 214–215.

Hunt, M. (1997), *How Science Takes Stock: The Story of Meta-Analysis.* New York: Russell Sage Foundation.

Iacobucci, D. (2005), "From the editor," *Journal of Consumer Research,* 32(1): 1–6.

JEP (2003), "Instructions to authors," *Journal of Educational Psychology,* 95(1): 201.

Kendall, P.C. (1997), "Editorial," *Journal of Consulting and Clinical Psychology,* 65(1): 3–5.

Kieffer, K.M., R.J. Reese, and B. Thompson (2001), "Statistical techniques employed in AERJ and JCP articles from 1988 to 1997: A methodological review," *Journal of Experimental Education,* 69(3): 280–309.

Kirk, R.E. (1996), "Practical significance: A concept whose time has come," *Educational and Psychological Measurement,* 56(5): 746–759.

Kirk, R.E. (2001), "Promoting good statistical practices: Some suggestions," *Educational and Psychological Measurement,* 61(2): 213–218.

Kirk, R.E. (2003), "The importance of effect magnitude," in S.F. Davis (editor), *Handbook of Research*

Methods in Experimental Psychology, Oxford, UK: Blackwell, 83–105.

Kolata, G.B. (1981), "Drug found to help heart attack survivors," *Science*, 214(13): 774–775.

La Greca, A.M. (2005), "Editorial," *Journal of Consulting and Clinical Psychology*, 73(1): 3–5.

Levant, R.F. (1992), "Editorial," *Journal of Family Psychology*, 6(1): 3–9.

Lustig, D. and D. Strauser (2004), "Editor's comment: Effect size and rehabilitation research," *Journal of Rehabilitation* 70(4): 3–5.

McCloskey, D.N. and S.T. Ziliak (1996), "The standard error of regressions," *Journal of Economic Literature*, 34(March): 97–114.

Melton, A. (1962), "Editorial," *Journal of Experimental Psychology*, 64(6): 553–557.

McLean, J.E. and A.S. Kaufman (2000), "Editorial: Statistical significance testing and Research in the Schools," *Research in the Schools*, 7(2).

Murphy, K.R. (1997), "Editorial," *Journal of Applied Psychology*, 82(1):3–5.

Pearson, K. (1905), "Report on certain enteric fever inoculation statistics," *British Medical Journal*, 2(2288): 1243–1246.

Rynes, S.L. (2007), "Editors afterword: Let's create a tipping point—what academics and practitioners can do, alone and together," *Academy of Management Journal*, 50(5): 1046–1054.

Shaver, J.M. (2006), "Interpreting empirical findings," *Journal of International Business Studies,* 37(4): 451–452.

Shaver, J.M. (2008), "Organizational significance," *Strategic Organization,* 6(2): 185–193.

Shaver, J.P. (1993), "What statistical significance testing is, and what it is not," *Journal of Experimental Education,* 61(4): 293–316.

Smith, M.L. and G.V. Glass (1977), "Meta-analysis of psychotherapy outcome studies," *American Psychologist,* 32(9): 752–760

Thompson, B. (1994), "Guidelines for authors," *Educational and Psychological Measurement,* 54, 837–847.

Thompson, B. (2002), "'Statistical,' 'practical,' and 'clinical': How many kinds of significance do counselors need to consider?" *Journal of Counseling and Development,* 80(1): 64–71.

Wilkinson, L. and the Taskforce on Statistical Inference (1999), "Statistical methods in psychology journals: Guidelines and expectations," *American Psychologist,* 54(8): 594–604.

Zedeck, S. (2003), "Editorial," *Journal of Applied Psychology.* 88(1): 3–5.

Ziliak, S.T. and D.N. McCloskey (2004), "Size matters: The standard error of regressions in the American Economic Review," *Journal of Socio-Economics,* 33(5): 527–546.